H O W
AMERICA
V I E W S   I T S
SCHOOLS

THE PDK/GALLUP POLLS, 1969-1994

BY
STANLEY ELAM

Published by
Phi Delta Kappa Educational Foundation
Bloomington, Indiana

Cover design by Victoria Voelker

Library of Congress Catalog Number 94-74369
ISBN 0-87367-473-1
Copyright © 1995 by Stanley Elam
Bloomington, Indiana

ACKNOWLEDGMENTS

I wish to acknowledge the invaluable help of several friends and colleagues in the preparation of this volume. First, thanks to Dean Roy D. Pea of the Northwestern University School of Education and Social Policy, who generously extended visiting scholar status so that I could use the university's library. Alec Gallup and his assistant, Sarah Van Allen, provided key data at certain points in the preparation of the manuscript. Neville Robertson, director of the Phi Delta Kappa Center for Dissemination of Innovative Programs, prepared the appendix description of PDK's PACE materials. Sheila Way and Debbie Webb, word-processing wizards at Phi Delta Kappa, converted my mangled typing into a neat manuscript. And Terri Hampton, publications secretary and jill of all trades at PDK, heeded all my cries for help.

Stanley Elam
Editor Emeritus, *Phi Delta Kappan*,
and Coordinator, Phi Delta Kappa Polls
August 1994

TABLE OF CONTENTS

INTRODUCTION

Abba Eben, the brilliant Israeli statesman, once remarked that "one who keeps his ear permanently glued to the ground will have neither grace of posture nor freedom of movement." It was clever phrase making, but the thought is only corollary to another maxim (author anonymous): "He who doesn't frequently test the wind runs the risk of being blown away."

Properly used, public polls and surveys can measure the sometimes fickle winds of public opinion with considerable accuracy, checking direction, intensity, and variability. And public opinion, in the last analysis, is what distinguishes the possible from the impossible in public education. I saw this repeatedly demonstrated in the struggle for collective bargaining in education during the Sixties. The movement succeeded in environments of public acceptance and failed where public approval was lacking. After all, we live in a democracy and the will of the people is our dictator.

I wrote a brief account of the origins of the Phi Delta Kappa/Gallup education poll for the September 1983 *Phi Delta Kappan*. Following is an excerpt from that account:

> If you had a sizable private fortune, would you study for a teaching certificate and specialize in counseling and guidance? Would you give a quarter of a million dollars for the legal defense of Chicago's largest youth gang, the Black P. Stone Nation? Would you devote a considerable portion of that fortune to the improvement of education?
>
> The late Charles F. Kettering II did all of these things.
>
> Like his grandfather, the legendary inventor, auto tycoon, and one-time country schoolteacher, young Charles had a consuming curiosity. (The first Charles F. Kettering wondered, for example, why grass is green. To find out, he set up a unit of the C.F. Kettering Foundation at Antioch College in nearby Yellow Springs to

1

study chlorophyll and photosynthesis.) But it did not lead him, as it had his grandfather, to build improved machines to serve humankind. Instead, it drove him to consider ways in which humankind itself can be improved. The grandson thought this transformation could be accomplished by proper education. Thus, when he became dissatisfied with the way the Charles F. Kettering Foundation of Dayton, Ohio, spent its money, he set up his own foundation, strictly to support education-related programs, and based it in Denver.

During its brief existence, CFK Ltd., the new foundation, developed three important education projects. One provided collegial inservice education for teams of school administrators throughout the nation. (Kettering had himself earned a master's degree in education at the University of Colorado after taking the B.A. in social studies at Dartmouth.) Another was a program for the improvement of school climate, a term coined by the foundation staff. A book on the topic, written by Edward A. Brainard for Phi Delta Kappa, was a best seller in the Seventies.

The third project was the annual Gallup poll of attitudes toward education, inaugurated in 1969.

When Kettering set up CFK Ltd., he asked Brainard, then director of the grants division of the Kettering Foundation, to serve as its president. Brainard's heart was in research. He was the former director of research and evaluation for the schools of Jefferson County outside of Denver, and while with the Kettering Foundation he saw to it that nearly $70,000 of the foundation's money went to Phi Delta Kappa in 1966 to set up a new research division at the Bloomington, Indiana, headquarters.

Brainard and Kettering were about the same age, and they worked well together. At one of their CFK Ltd. planning sessions, Brainard suggested that they ask George Gallup, Sr., then a member of the Kettering Foundation Board of Trustees, what he thought of the idea of an annual education poll. No sooner said than done.

As it turned out, Gallup proved to be at least as enthusiastic about improving education as the two young foundation executives. He had been a university professor himself before pioneering the development of scientific polling in the 1930s. Several members of his immediate family were also teachers. So the senior Gallup (two sons help with the business) quoted CFK Ltd. a ridiculously low figure for conducting the poll. Gallup has devoted a great deal of his time to the poll ever since; he insists on analyzing and presenting the annual results of the survey himself — on one occasion even performing this chore while hospitalized with a broken leg. Five years ago [1978] he helped Phi Delta

2

Kappa develop its PACE (Polling Attitudes of the Community on Education) materials for surveying local education sentiment — and charged nothing for the service. [See Appendix for a description of PACE.]

My own involvement with the Gallup polls began when I summarized the first poll report for the November 1969 KAPPAN. Shortly thereafter, Brainard asked whether Phi Delta Kappa would be interested in publishing the entire text of the next survey report in the fraternity journal, which had a circulation of about 80,000 [it is over 150,000 in 1994]. I said yes, and the Gallup poll has been an annual KAPPAN feature ever since.

Unfortunately, Charles Kettering II did not live to see the education poll become a national institution. He died in December 1971. Trying to rescue the family dog from being run down by a car, he himself was hit and fatally injured. He had just celebrated his fortieth birthday.

Two and one-half years later, CFK Ltd. completed its program and was discontinued. For a time it looked as if the poll might die for lack of funds. But Brainard and B. Frank Brown, the innovative Florida educator then directing the Institute for Development of Educational Activities (/I/D/E/A/) for the Kettering Foundation, were determined to save it. Brainard went to the Ford Foundation and obtained funding for one year. The next year the Kettering Foundation offered to pick up the tab and continued doing so until 1981, when declining income forced retrenchment. At this point Phi Delta Kappa, with a grant from the Lilly Endowment, stepped in as sponsor as well as publisher. For the first time this year [1983], Phi Delta Kappa is bearing the full cost of the poll, which is something over $40,000.

For many years the poll's circulation and influence have been enhanced by media summaries and by reports in various education journals other than the *Kappan*. At one time PDK shipped as many as 75,000 poll report reprints annually, on hundreds of orders from around the country. The Educational Press Association of America sent reprints to each of its more than 600 members. A poll report has been reprinted in the *Congressional Record*. It was even quoted in *A Nation at Risk*. Under the guidance of PDK Executive Director Lowell Rose, national press conferences have been held in August since 1985 to release report findings.

The PDK/Gallup polls usually are taken in April, but preparation begins at least six months earlier. Although questions have been generated in a variety of ways, the prime consideration in the final selection is a question's promise of giving useful information to education practitioners and particularly to policy makers, including state legislators and congressmen.

In recent years an advisory panel of 15 to 20 knowledgeable educators at various levels and with many specialties has been assembled annually to submit question suggestions. These ideas are edited, categorized, and consolidated into a list, usually of about 100 questions, which is resubmitted to the panel for ranking in accord with the question's promise of yielding useful information. Because of the strong emphasis on tracking opinion trends on perennial problems and issues, at least one-fourth of the questions asked in a given poll have been asked at least once in prior polls. This means that only 25 to 30 questions asked in any year are new. Only about 40 questions can be asked in any one poll, because of financial limitations and because Gallup interviews, for best results, must be limited to no more than 30 minutes.

In the next step, the question list is submitted to the Gallup Organization, usually in March, for final screening, refinement, and (sometimes) field testing. The task of the Gallup professionals is, first, to make sure that the wording and intent of each question is clear. Questions cannot be overly technical. Professional jargon must be eliminated. And, so far as that is possible, questions must be "unloaded." That is, sources of bias are identified and eliminated.

Much public polling is of the "hired gun" variety. The pollster is expected to predetermine results by introducing bias that favors the client. A Ross Perot poll done in March 1993 is a textbook example of how readily this can be done. The poll asked, "Should laws be passed to eliminate all possibilities of special interests giving large sums of money to [political] candidates?" Ninety-nine percent of those responding answered yes. But in an alternate form, rephrased by an independent polling concern, only 40% favored limits on contributions. The alternate form: "Do groups have a right to contribute to the candidate they support?"

With exaggeration, Mike Royko, the ascerbic *Chicago Tribune* columnist, makes the point even clearer. Royko was discussing public opinion poll questions about people's willingness to have their taxes raised. His alternative question forms:

1. Would you be willing to pay a little more to help your children and grandchildren have a brighter future?
2. Do you believe it is your patriotic duty to entrust your money to a pack of moochers, double-talkers, and dead beats?

In the pages that follow, I have attempted to relate selected findings of the annual polls to the Phi Delta Kappa ideal: the promotion and improvement of free public education as an instrument of democracy. The public schools belong to the people. Through the polls, we are listening to the people.

Editor's note: Readers who are interested in detailed annual reports may purchase *The Gallup/Phi Delta Kappa Polls of Attitudes Toward the Public Schools, 1969-1988: A 20-Year Compilation and Educational History*. Individual copies of the annual reports that have been published in the *Phi Delta Kappan* since 1988 also are available. Contact: Phi Delta Kappa, 408 North Union Avenue, P.O. Box 789, Bloomington, IN 47402-0789. Phone (812) 339-1156.

CHAPTER 1

A QUESTION OF CONFIDENCE

The cover story in the 19 April 1993 edition of *Newsweek*, titled "A Nation Still at Risk," quoted David Gardner as saying, "What I see is a slow, steady erosion of public regard for the public schools and in some respects a psychological abandonment."

"Gardner," said *Newsweek*, "worries about the perception that the schools are not salvageable."

This is the kind of pretentious, hysterical hyperbole that made President Reagan's Excellence in Education Commission report, *A Nation at Risk: The Imperative for Educational Reform*, such a media sensation when it appeared ten years earlier. It was David Gardner who chaired the Excellence Commission at the beginning of his nine-year term as president of the University of California at Berkeley.

As *Newsweek* noted, "*A Nation at Risk* could have been just another dull report, one of thousands issued annually by faceless bureaucrats and academics." But no. It proved to be a landmark in the history of American school reform. It was a forceful manifesto eschewing sober academic language. It predicted that the country could soon be swallowed by a "rising tide of mediocrity." It detected "a widespread public perception that something is seriously amiss in our educational system." It even hinted at conspiracy: "If an unfriendly foreign power had attempted to impose on America the mediocre educational performance that exists today, we might well have viewed it as an act of war."

I don't know who was responsible for these fevered phrases, but I tip my hat to his polemic power.

What I really wanted to know when I read *Newsweek's* tenth anniversary issue was this: Where did Gardner find the data that persuaded him Americans are losing faith in their public schools, so much so that these schools "may not be salvageable"? What lay behind those apocalyptic words?

7

So I asked Mr. Gardner for more background than a news magazine is willing to publish (especially when it runs a 5" x 6" photo of the speaker).

Many weeks later, and only after resorting to genteel blackmail, I received a response that cited no research but suggested that evidence of erosion of public regard for the public schools is ubiquitous and that Gardner's opinion was drawn from "decades of working with legislators, members of Congress, school boards, teachers and their organizations, and with leaders in the minority and corporate communities." Did he listen to anyone in the general American public? That group tells a different story in the PDK/Gallup attitude/opinion polls.

I suggested to Gardner that California's one-sided referendum vote against vouchers in November 1993 may be considered evidence that the people in his state, like those of Oregon and Colorado, have not given up on their public schools. In response he said, "The fact that the initiative was on the ballot at all, together with the support it received, is evidence of something!" I agree. But evidence of what?

I focus on Gardner only to illustrate a pernicious syndrome. I'm indebted to Gerald Bracey's first *Phi Delta Kappan* report on the state of the nation's public schools (September 1991, pp. 105-17) for these further examples of myopic pessimism:

- When President Bush announced America 2000, he said, "We've moved beyond the days of issuing reports about the dismal state of our schools."
- The opening sentence in Edward Fiske's 1991 book, *Smart Schools, Smart Kids: Why Do Some Schools Work?*, was, "It's no secret that America's public schools are failing."
- Chester Finn, former assistant secretary for research and improvement in the Department of Education, recently said: "[These] examples [of educational shortcomings] are so familiar we're tempted not to pay them much heed. Why make ourselves miserable?"
- And at the opening session of the annual conference on assessment sponsored by the American Educational Research Association, Lauren Resnick, former president of the AERA and co-director of a foundation-funded effort to establish national standards and examinations, said, "We all know how terrible we are."

Another illustration of the syndrome comes from the mercifully forgotten report of the President's Commission for a National Agenda for the Eighties, which said, "Continued failure by the schools to perform their traditional role adequately, together with a failure to respond to the emergency needs of the Eighties, may have disastrous consequences in such areas as national defense, technology, and productivity."

Phi Delta Kappa/Gallup polls have been sampling public opinion about U.S. public schools for 26 years. One of the concerns of the professional fraternity — which is dedicated to research, service, and leadership in education — has been to examine, in as objective and scientific a manner as stratified random sampling permits, the many dimensions of the people's confidence in the ability of the public schools to do the job entrusted to them. While more than a score of questions have probed this issue, three were considered so crucial that they have been asked annually in recent years:

1. Students are often given the grades A, B, C, D, and FAIL to denote the quality of their work. Suppose the public schools themselves, in this community, were graded in the same way. What grade would you give the public schools here? (Asked since 1974)
2. How about the public schools in the nation as a whole? What grade would you give the public schools nationally — A, B, C, D, or FAIL? (Asked since 1982)
3. Using the A, B, C, D, FAIL scale again, what grade would you give the school your oldest child attends? (Asked since 1986 of parents of public school children)

Nationwide, parents grade the schools their own children attend just short of B, and they have done so every year since 1986, when the question was first asked in the PDK/Gallup polls. In my judgment, this response reflects a remarkable achievement by the public schools, laboring as they do under increasingly formidable handicaps. Those handicaps include a doubling of the number of children living in poverty over the past decade or so and the virtual breakdown of the nuclear family.

What we have here are people all over the U.S. making judgments about the quality of a school they know well, partly through the eyes of their children, often through personal contacts with teachers, staff, and administrators as well as other parents, and usually through attendance at school-sponsored affairs of various kinds. For example, the 1994 PDK/Gallup poll shows that 87% of parents reported consulting, person-to-person, with teachers or administrators about their children every year. Nearly 80% attended a school play, concert, or athletic event. These are primary sources.

Slightly lower marks are given to the public schools by other respondents, ranked in descending order:

9

- local schools as viewed by public school parents (asked since 1974);
- the nation's schools as viewed by public school parents (asked since 1982);
- local schools as viewed by respondents without children in school (asked since 1974);
- the nation's schools as viewed by respondents without children in school (asked since 1982).

Although lower than the first group, all four successive groups of respondents give the public schools marks in the B/C range.

The lowest marks are given for schools nationally. These groups know about schools on a nationwide basis from *secondary* sources, including the local newspapers and radio and television. Thus the information and opinions they receive have been filtered by gatekeepers whose primary concern and motivation is to gain attention and sell products and services. After all, we live in a consumer society.

And how do the media gain attention? As everyone knows, by reporting — often exaggerating — the singular, the aberrant, the bizarre, and the negative. Media treatment of education in America is a topic worthy of extended analysis. While I will not attempt it here, the reader can find an excellent analysis in George Kaplan's *Images of Education: The Mass Media's Version of America's Schools* (1992); in Paul Woodring's *The Persistent Problems of Education* (1983); and in Gerald Bracey's four annual reports in the *Phi Delta Kappan* (October 1991, 1992, 1993, and 1994). Woodring summed up the situation thus: "With occasional brilliant exceptions, media coverage of education is poor in quality and inadequate in scope. All too often, the facts are misinterpreted and analysis is misleading." As editor of the *Saturday Review* education supplement for six years, Woodring knew whereof he spoke.

A compilation by the Washington-based Center for Media and Public Affairs for the 30-month period from February 1987 through July 1989 revealed that the three major TV networks ran a total of 350 stories on education-related matters, or about 1% of the 36,000 pieces on all subjects that aired during that time. Of the 350, approximately 150 had little to do with the schools (items, for example, on Oliver North as a commencement speaker and national service as an emerging issue), while many of the remaining 200 or so fastened on such continuing but essentially peripheral stories as student demonstrations at Gallaudet College, the wit and wisdom of William Bennett, or the plight of a child with AIDS.

George Kaplan, writing in *Images of Education: The Mass Media's Version of America's Schools*, concluded, "When sophisticated polls repeatedly demonstrate our dependence on TV as a central source of information on public issues, it is folly [for education leaders] to ignore or ridicule it."

One of the best recent, brief treatments of newspaper coverage of education appeared in *Education Week* for 16 February 1994 under the title, "Are Newspapers Missing the Beat?" Author Mark Walsh summarized the indictments of past coverage but found some cause for optimism. Interviews with education reporters, newspaper editors, media analysts, and educators, he said, indicate that, having taken to heart what the media critics say, some newspapers "are doing something about it." Walsh reported several instances of excellent coverage of education stories and probes of educational issues. But he noted,

> One of the perennial problems facing the public schools concerns public relations. The media are prone to limit their coverage of [the schools] to what journalists describe as 'spot' news. . . . Unfortunately, these stories usually concern vandalism, drugs, absenteeism, theft of school property, attacks on teachers, and the like. 'Good news' is difficult to find and report.
>
> Consequently, the public receives a distorted picture of schools and tends to regard them as blackboard jungles.

The people themselves are not pleased with media coverage of education. In 1969, 65% of all poll respondents and 77% of all parents of public school children said they would like to learn more about their local public schools. Asked in the 1977 poll if they thought "the media (newspapers, TV, and radio) give a fair and accurate picture of the public schools" in their communities, more than one-third (36%) said no. And they were full of suggestions for improvement. The more frequent suggestions dwelt on the need for positive news, such as interesting things the schools are doing to achieve their educational goals. Specific suggestions included:

- Reporters should be sent into the schoolrooms to see what goes on there.
- It would be interesting to find out about all of the different courses that are offered.
- Why don't the media tell us about the standing of the local schools — how well they do in comparison with private schools and with schools in nearby cities?

- I should like to know more about the changes that are being introduced and why.
- The media report on the school budget, but they never tell in detail just where our tax dollars are spent.
- Outstanding students should be written up and praised the way top athletes are.

Today's most debilitating myth is the one that Mr. Gardner appears to have accepted as gospel, that public education, as an institution, is a goner. He has bought the thesis that maverick education critic Myron Lieberman propounds in *Public Education: An Autopsy* (1993). Many social and political leaders whose motives can hardly be questioned have accepted this same myth. Even educators who should know better are victimized.

Poll respondents do not generally reflect this pessimism. However, a significant number of parents, about 30 in a sample of 431 (or four million of the 60 million U.S. parents with children in public schools) do have little or no confidence in the job their schools are doing. They awarded D's or F's.

Four million, while only 7% of the total, is a sizable group. Poll data give us some clues to the identity of these dissatisfied clients. They tend to live in cities of one million or more. More often than not, they are among the nation's growing racial and ethnic minorities. Only rarely do wealthier or better-educated public school parents give their children's schools D's or F's. One reason for these facts is obvious: Better educated and affluent parents can move to districts with better schools; by and large, the poor cannot. Moreover, advantaged parents fight to maintain and improve their community schools and have the means to do so.

David Gardner's intuition told him that the trend should be toward lower grades after 1983. Actually, the grades trend upward, even when given by adults with no children in school.

Public Confidence in All Institutions

The Gallup Organization has conducted other studies apart from its service to Phi Delta Kappa, of course. These studies show, by and large, that people have lost a great deal of confidence in many public and private institutions that serve them. We live in a cynical era. In 1993 public confidence ranked the following institutions in descending order of confidence:

the military
the church, or organized religion
the public schools
newspapers
Congress
television

I would illustrate this point as follows:

First, public confidence in all but one of the six institutions, three of them private sector, one public, dropped rather seriously between 1973 and 1993. The only winner was the military, which was the beneficiary of a massive Cold War buildup during this period, particularly after Ronald Reagan took office as President in 1981. And the military proved itself, first in Grenada, then in Panama, and then much more emphatically and dramatically in the Persian Gulf War.

One wonders how confidence in the military and the public schools might have tracked differently had a President exploited the public sentiment detected in a question asked in the PDK/Gallup polls for 1982, 1984, 1988, and 1991. That question was: "In determining America's strength in the future — say, 25 years from now — how important do you feel each of the following factors will be — very important, fairly important, not too important, or not at all important?" The results are shown in Table 1.

Table 1. Determining America's strength.

	Very Imp.		Fairly Imp.		Not too Imp.		Not at all Imp.		Don't Know	
	'82 %	'91 %	'82 %	'91 %	'82 %	'91 %	'82 %	'91 %	'82 %	'91 %
1. Developing the best educational system in the world	84	89	13	9	1	1	-	-	2	1
2. Developing the most efficient industrial production system in the world	66	59	26	32	3	5	-	-	4	4
3. Building the strongest military force in the world	47	41	37	39	11	15	2	3	3	2

Although the 1991 poll was taken only weeks after victory for the Allied forces in the Gulf War, people were more firmly convinced than ever, in that year, that developing the best educational system in the world is more important for America's strength in the future than building the strongest military force.

Second, public schools trail only the church and the military among the six institutions. From high confidence in 1973 — 58% of respondents expressing either a great deal of confidence or quite a lot of confidence in the public schools — the level has tumbled to 39%. This has to be discouraging to public school educators. But what about public confidence in newspapers? Newspapers, starting from a much lower point, lost 41% over the same period. Television lost even more — in percentage terms, nearly 60%. In fact, both Congress and TV almost drop off the chart.

Changing Attitudes

This chapter would be incomplete without a report on the findings from an attitude question asked sporadically and in slightly different forms over the poll's history. The question took this form in 1973: "In recent years has your overall attitude toward the public schools in your community become more favorable or less favorable?" In the total response, 32% said more favorable, 36% less favorable, and 23% no change. Nine percent gave no answer.

Demographic breakdowns show significant differences by category of respondent. Of the 620 public school parents in the sample, 42% said more favorable, while only 31% said less favorable. By contrast, of the 928 parents with no children in school, 25% said more favorable and 38% less favorable.

In small cities (25,000 to 50,000), 48% said more favorable, 27% less favorable, and 21% no change. But in large cities (500,000 or more), the figures were approximately reversed: 28% more favorable, 37% less favorable, 26% no change.

In the same 1973 poll, people also were asked, "As you look over your own elementary and high school education, is it your impression that children today get a better or a worse education than you did?" The national totals: better, 61%; worse, 20%; no difference, 11%; no opinion, 8%. Those respondents in a position to be best informed — parents with children in the public schools — said "better" by a 3 to 1 margin. They liked what they took to be a broadened curriculum in contemporary schools, better facilities and equipment, better teaching methods, better qualified teachers, and greater equality of opportunity for all students.

The second of these two questions was repeated in 1979 (and in January 1994, in a Gallup poll not sponsored by Phi Delta Kappa). The results show a considerable slippage in favorable responses between 1972 and 1979 but little change from 1979 to 1994.

In 1979 people in smaller communities (under 50,000) were most likely to believe their children were getting a better education than they themselves did (47% better, 36% worse). And there were distinct regional differences. Respondents in Western states (dominated by California) were least satisfied: 27% said better, 51% worse. People in the South: 47% said better, 40% worse.

College-educated respondents were more likely to take the negative view (36% better, 46% worse) than were respondents with only an elementary or high school education.

Interestingly, in this 1979 poll nonwhites were more likely than whites to believe their children were getting a better education than they themselves did (nonwhite, 49%; white, 39%). At first glance, these percentages seem to contradict the fact, already noted, that the nonwhite category includes a segment highly dissatisfied with their public schools. Impoverished minorities are often poorly served, as Jonathan Kozol made abundantly clear in his book, *Savage Inequalities*. At the same time, there are many recent immigrants in the nonwhite category — mainly Hispanics and Asians — who are comparing U.S. schools with those of the Third World from which they fled. Also, many older blacks in this category compare the schools they now know with separate but unequal schools of their past. Finally, the growing black middle class is abandoning the inner city for suburban amenities, including better schools. Thus within the nonwhite category there are several subgroups that believe their children are getting a better education than they themselves did.

That U.S. public schools are failing has become a media cliché. Many school critics and media pundits have assumed that the public has bought this cliché and is ready to abandon the defining features of democratic public education, painfully developed over 150 years of history. The facts of the matter, as revealed in Phi Delta Kappa/Gallup polls, are these:

- Public confidence in public education did decline somewhat between 1974 and 1983, as did confidence in many U.S. institutions immediately following Watergate. However, in general the public is well-satisfied with the job the public schools are doing. This satisfaction is particularly strong among that segment of the public in a position to hold informed opinions: the parents of public school children. After 1983, public confidence in the public schools, as measured by the grades people give these schools for the job they are doing, has risen in the face of generally negative and often misleading media reports and a declining proportion of parents in the adult population.

- Confidence in public education is lowest among groups who are being poorest served: inner-city blacks, other minorities, and people living in poverty, including the rural poor. It is noteworthy that since 1973, during a time in which Americans over age 40 became our richest generation in history, the percentage of American youths living below the poverty level rose by 51%. Four million more young people grow up in poverty today than 20 years ago (U.S. Bureau of the Census 1993). (See Chapter 2 on inequalities in school funding and public reaction to them.)
- Nationally, the schools rank with the church and the military as the most highly regarded U.S. institutions, ahead of newspapers; television; the courts; federal, state, and local government; big business; unions; and Congress.

Educators and education policy makers should be gratified by these facts, but not complacent. As this summary of past education polls will show, the public is well aware of many of the current challenges to public education and welcomes reform.

CHAPTER 2

MORE WILL THAN WALLET?

In 1993 inadequate funding emerged in many people's perception as the number-one problem for their local public schools. It was listed by one-fifth of all respondents and by one-fourth of all adults with children in the public schools. (Drug abuse was second with 16% in 1993, after several years at the top of the list.)

This was the first time since 1971 that the public agreed (albeit not to the same extent) with education professionals on the salience of financial problems for the schools. Poll findings among the Phi Delta Kappa membership are probably typical of professional opinion; and in 1987, 60% of the fraternity's members identified funding as a major public school problem. Fourteen percent of the general public mentioned inadequate education funding as a major problem.

In general, poll findings suggest that school finance is an area of considerable confusion for most lay people. U.S. political leaders have added more than their share to this confusion. For example, John Sununu, speaking shortly before the nation's governors adopted six national education goals in 1989, declared, "We spend twice as much [on education] as the Japanese and about 40% more than all of the other major industrial countries of the world." Sununu's remarks were widely quoted, and thus the President's right-hand man perpetuated a misconception that has pervaded public discussion of school issues for more than a decade. In fact, the U.S. does *not* lead the world in K-12 education expenditures (Berliner 1993).

In 1990 the Economic Policy Institute of Washington, D.C., issued an authoritative study by M. Edith Rasell and Lawrence Miskel, *Short-changing Education*, showing that in 1988 dollars the U.S. ranked ninth among 16 industrialized nations in per-pupil expenditures for grades K-12. The U.S. spent 40% less than Germany, 30% less than Japan, and 51% less than Switzerland. In 1985, as shown in Table 2, we were fifteenth among 17 industrialized nations in spending on grades K-12 as a percentage of gross national product, which is probably the best measure of a nation's commitment to education. The latest (1992) report of the Organization for Economic Cooperation and Development (OECD), *Education at a Glance*, placed the U.S. behind 12 other nations in the percentage of gross domestic product devoted to public and private education.

Table 2. International comparisons of education expenditures, 1985.

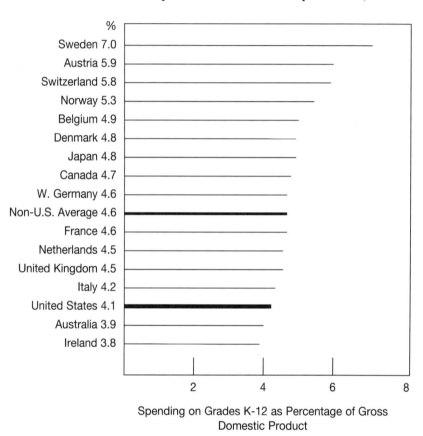

Spending on Grades K-12 as Percentage of Gross
Domestic Product

Source: M. Edith Rasell and Lawrence Mishel, *Shortchanging Education* (Washington, D.C.: Economic Policy Institute, 1990), p.5.

During their terms of office, former Department of Education Secretaries William Bennett, Lauro Cavazos, and Lamar Alexander all alleged that we spend more on education than do our economic rivals, Germany and Japan. This is true only if the cost of higher education is included in the total. We spend much more on higher education because we have two to three times as many people in college per 100,000 population as do most of the other industrialized countries, including Germany and Japan. (One result of our emphasis on higher education is that 40% of all research articles in the world are published by U.S. authors; no other nation produces more than 3%. And the U.S. leads all nations in the number of Nobel Prize winners it produces. [See Iris Rotberg, "Measuring Up to the Competition: A Few Hard Questions," in *Technos*, Winter 1990].)

Improving Schools by Throwing Money at Them

Despite the political smokescreens and endless repetition of the cliché, "You can't improve the schools by throwing money at them," most people have arrived at two very important conclusions about school finance. Neither suggests that people have accepted the cliché. These are the people's beliefs, as revealed in the 1993 poll:

1. Differences in funding from state to state and from district to district are largely responsible for the uneven quality of public education in America.

To obtain this finding, Gallup interviewers first determined that a majority of the respondents knew that the quality of education and the funding of education differ greatly from school district to school district and from state to state; people generally answered either "a great deal" or "quite a lot." Then interviewers asked for opinions on this question: How much does the amount of money spent on a public school student's education affect the quality of his or her education? Sixty-eight percent answered "a great deal" (38%) or "quite a lot" (30%). Only 25% answered "not too much" and 5% "not at all."

Twenty years earlier, in the 1973 poll, this question was asked: "In some school districts, about $600 is spent per child per school year; some school districts spend more than $1,200. Do you think this additional expenditure of money makes a great deal of difference in the achievement or progress of students, or little difference?" Thirty-nine percent of the national sample said "a great deal," but 38% said "little difference." Only 10% said "no difference," while 13% gave no response. Parents of public school children were not quite so tentative; 45% said the additional expenditure would make a great deal of difference, 36% said little difference, and 8% said no difference.

19

It would appear that, in the 20 years between the 1973 poll and the 1993 poll, people came to understand somewhat better the connection between school expenditures and school effectiveness.

2. Not only do people believe that more must be done to improve the quality of public schools in the poorer states and poorer communities, but they are willing to pay more taxes in order to do it.

This is the more significant response. Respondents were almost unanimous (90% yes, 8% no) in expressing the opinion that "more must be done." A solid majority (68%) said they would be willing to pay more taxes to improve public schools in the poorer states and communities. Thirty percent said no, and 2% didn't respond.

Admittedly, giving a politically correct answer to a pollster who is asking questions about education is considerably different from signing a check to pay more taxes or voting for someone whose platform is equalization of resources for the public schools. But these 1993 poll answers are evidence that the spirit of fairness is alive and well in America. It is also evidence that people have not paid much attention to that strand of research suggesting that school quality, or at least school effectiveness, is not greatly influenced by added expenditures.

David C. Berliner (1993) identifies several factors that debunk what he calls "the myth that money is unrelated to the outcomes of schooling." Among these factors are the following:

- States that had spent the most on their schools had produced the citizens with the highest incomes.
- Higher salaries attract teaching candidates with higher academic abilities and keep teachers in the profession longer.
- Data on millions of students in 900 Texas districts were examined longitudinally from 1986 to 1990 and revealed that 1) teachers' academic proficiency explains 20% to 25% of the variation across districts in students' average scores on academic achievement tests, and 2) teachers with more years of experience have students with higher test scores, lower dropout rates, and higher rates of taking the SAT.
- Once class size exceeds 18 students (according to the same Texas longitudinal study), each student over that number is associated with a drop in district academic achievement.
- Most of the real increases in education expenditures over the last 20 years have been the result of increased costs for transportation, health care, and special education.

20

Are the People Willing to Pay?

Over the years, the PDK/Gallup polls have explored many facets of school finance. In the remainder of this chapter I will summarize only certain significant findings and trace certain trends that appear to be of most interest.

The very first poll asked for a response to this question: "Suppose the local public schools said they needed much more money. As you feel at this time, would you vote to raise taxes for this purpose, or would you vote against raising taxes for this purpose?" The question was repeated in eight subsequent polls. (See Table 3.)

Table 3. Raising taxes to pay for schools.

	1969 %		1970 %		1971 %		1972 %		1981 %		1983 %		1984 %		1985 %		1986 %	
	Nation	Parents	Nation	Parents	Nation	Parents	Nation	Parents	Nation	Parents	Nation	Parents	Nation	Parents	Nation	Parents	Nation	Parents
Would vote for	45	51	37	43	40	44	36	37	30	36	39	48	41	54	38	46	37	45
Would vote against	49	44	56	53	52	49	56	56	60	58	52	45	47	38	52	47	52	46
Don't know, no resp.	6	5	7	4	8	7	8	7	10	6	9	7	12	8	10	7	11	9

Note that in only three years — 1969, 1983, and 1984 — were even public school parents willing to pay more taxes because "the schools said they needed much more money." The real meaning of these findings became clear only when, in 1983, a related question was asked: "Would you be willing to pay more taxes to raise the standards of education in the United States?" The favorable margin was a convincing 58% yes to 33% no, with 9% not responding.

There is more than a subtle difference between increasing taxes because "the public schools say they need much more money" and increasing taxes "to raise the standards of education in the United States." In responding to the first question, many people no doubt thought, "Well, of course government agencies always want 'much more money.' I'm not about to say yes unless and until I know just what the 'much more money' is for." "Raising standards" in the public schools is exactly what the people want, a fact amply documented in literally dozens of other poll responses in this series.

Following are several additional points that give a sense of the way people think about school finance issues:

Poll respondents consistently have opposed what is still a general practice: reliance on local property taxes for much of public school funding. As early as 1970, 1971, and 1972, for example, they favored by a 5 to 3 majority increasing state sources of income so that local real estate taxes could be lowered. It is useful to note that, on the average, states today pay about half the cost of public education, while local governments provide something over 44% and the federal government only 6%. But the states vary in their contribution, from a high of 91% in Hawaii to a low of 7.3% in New Hampshire (Jordan and Lyons 1992).

People generally have opposed encroachment of federal authority on local school decision making. In 1977 they approved, by a better than 2 to 1 margin, the suggestion that local authorities be allowed to determine how federal money earmarked for specific school purposes should be spent. But in 1991, people favored, by more than a 2 to 1 margin, court action that would equalize district-to-district differences in school funding.

Asked how they would reduce spending in times of tight government budgets, people were very reluctant to reduce the number of teachers employed. For example, 78% opposed this form of cost-cutting in the 1991 poll. But in that same recession year, the idea of a freeze on all school salaries was approved by 47% and opposed by 46%. Also, 73% liked the idea of reducing the number of administrators and only 19% opposed it. In fact, reducing the number of administrators is the all-time most popular cost-cutting method, approved by 50% in 1971, by 72% in 1976, and by 71% in 1982. (Gallup's interviewers were forbidden to explain that teacher salaries constitute some 80% of the typical district's total operating expenses. Thus in many larger districts, increasing class size by one student could "save" more money than the elimination of 80% of the administrative staff.)

In general people believe, by a sizable majority, in raising teacher salaries. For example, the 1991 poll showed 54% in favor, 32% opposed.

In 1991, 55% of respondents said they would be willing to pay higher taxes to fund free preschool programs.

In 1992 people favored (55% to 35%) extending the school year by 30 days, a change that could cost as much as $50 billion a year nationwide. (The poll did not probe whether respondents were aware of the potential cost.)

In 1993 a majority (59% to 38%) said they were willing to pay taxes to make child-care centers available for all preschool children as part of the public school program.

In 1993 people said they would like for the public schools to provide health and social services to students. These costly programs were approved by overwhelming margins: exams to detect sight and hearing defects (92% yes), free or low-cost lunches (87% yes), inoculations (84% yes), and after-school care for children of working parents (62% yes).

President Bush, a self-styled Education President, complained when confronted with demands for more federal education funds, "We have more will than wallet." This chapter shows that the public has never subscribed to this pessimistic view. People regard good education as a necessary and profitable investment, more productive than industrial development or a strong military. And they believe that more money will buy better quality schools, with higher student achievement the ultimate goal.

CHAPTER 3

EDUCATIONAL CHANGE

Remember performance contracting? I do — but with some embarrassment. I was one of the educators who thought, a quarter-century ago, that performance contracting held some promise for education, combining as it did the principles of competition and accountability — no results, no pay — with the efficiencies of technology.

I drove to Texarkana, which straddles the border of Texas and Arkansas, on April Fool's Day, 1970, to see what Loyd Dorsett's people had wrought in the schools of that small city. Dorsett was a leading practitioner of the new movement. Three days later I was at home writing "The Age of Accountability Dawns in Texarkana" for the June *Kappan*. In the article, I noted that at least 25 other U.S. school systems, including those of such major cities as Detroit, Dallas, Portland (Ore.), and San Diego, had now jumped on the performance contracting bandwagon.

Texarkana school officials had advertised for proposals and bids on a project funded mainly with federal dropout-prevention money. Dorsett beat out 112 other private groups for the contract. I was impressed by all that his methods and his teaching machines had accomplished in less than a year, and I found preliminary achievement figures encouraging.

But only two years later the performance contracting innovation was, for all intents and purposes, defunct. A contributing factor was the failure of the Texarkana experiment. More than the Hawthorne Effect had been at work. Some of Dorsett's overzealous employees had been teaching the answers to questions asked in the standardized tests used to determine payments to Dorsett. Performance contracting projects in other settings had bombed noisily or folded quietly when federal money dried up.

In the quarter-century covered by the PDK/Gallup polls, performance contracting was just one of dozens of efforts — some sound and successful, others feckless and doomed — to change or transform schooling in the United States. In some quarters, education has a reputation for susceptibility to any fad that comes along. But most education innovations do not die in the crib, as performance contracting did. More innovations are generated from within the profession than from outside, and many do succeed. Those that have many different sources of support are the most likely to survive. Certainly, many educators work hard at reform; and some make their professional name as change agents.

On the other hand, how often is it said that a visitor from a contemporary elementary school classroom who walked into one from the 1890s would find few real differences apart from the color of the chalkboard and the picture of the President on the wall?

These contrasting perceptions of change were reflected in answers to a question first asked in the 1970 poll: "Do you feel that the local public schools are not interested enough in trying new ways and methods, or are they *too ready* to try new ideas?" The question was asked again in 1974. The results are shown in Table 4.

Table 4. Local Schools trying new ideas.

	1970 %	1974 %
Not interested enough	20	24
Too ready to try new ideas	21	20
Just about right	32	32
Don't know	27	24

Although "just about right" won in both years, there were significant numbers on the opposing sides. Interestingly enough, in the 1970 poll a sample of high school juniors and seniors was asked the same question. These youngsters were more than twice as impatient as their elders: 43% said the schools were "not interested enough in trying new ideas." Only 19% of the students said "too ready." In the adult poll, younger and better-educated respondents were most likely to favor trying new ideas in the schools. The same finding is true, in general, of responses to questions about specific changes.

For example, is the U.S. public ready to change its priorities in the education of children? The PDK/Gallup polls give us some hints, and the short answer is "Yes, but reluctantly." A good illustration of this reluctance appears in the *Phi Delta Kappan* report of the 1993 poll:

Over a 25-year period, these polls have shown that the U.S. public usually favors a change or innovation in the public schools if the change promises improvement. [Forty of 53 suggested changes were approved by sizable margins in the first 20 polls.] But it has taken the public nearly a decade to recognize that the traditional nine-month school year may no longer suffice in a post-industrial, knowledge-driven, and increasingly global society.

Beginning in 1982, the following question was periodically asked in the [polls]: In some nations, students attend school as many as 240 days a year as compared to about 180 in the U.S. How do you feel about extending the public school year in this community by 30 days, making the school year about 210 days or 10 months long? Do you favor or oppose this idea?

The proposal finally gained majority approval in 1991, as the table below shows:

Extend School Year 30 Days

	1992 %	1991 %	1984 %	1983 %	1982 %
Favor	55	51	44	40	37
Oppose	35	42	50	49	53
Don't know	10	7	6	11	10

In the current poll, the question was put differently. The question:

Some public schools in the nation have increased the amount of time students spend in school by extending the school year or school day. Do you favor or oppose increasing the amount of time students spend in the public schools in your community?

	National Totals %	No Children In School %	Public School Parents %	Nonpublic School Parents %
Favor	52	53	50	54
Oppose	47	45	49	43
Don't know	1	2	1	3

Responses to Change

At the close of this chapter is a 25-year compilation of more than 100 "changes" showing the percentages of respondents favoring and opposing them.

B. Othanel Smith and Donald Orlosky wrote an insightful research-based article for the March 1972 *Kappan* titled "Educational Change: Its Origins and Characteristics." It reported on 63 broad changes attempted during the preceding 75 years. The authors determined that 24 of the 63 changes they studied had been installed successfully and had permeated the nation's education system.

Forty-nine of the 63 changes originated within school systems; only 14 came from without. But some of the latter were (and are) important; for example, adult education, compensatory education, compulsory attendance, desegregation, driver education, environmental education, Head Start, nursery schools, vocational and technical education, and special education.

Successful post-1950 ideas usually involved school organization and administration. A change that requires teachers to abandon an existing practice and displace it with a new one risks defeat. So do changes that require education personnel to relinquish power or that cast doubt on educator roles. Also, the lack of a diffusion system will lead to aborted change.

Smith and Orlosky recognized, but did not emphasize, the importance of public acceptance or support of proposed changes. (They used the term "social" rather than "public" support.) They *did* emphasize that the education system in a dynamic society cannot remain stagnant. "We should expect changes to be proposed that will greatly alter the school system, since the United States itself is undergoing rapid change," they concluded.

Smith and Orlosky offered 14 principles to guide those who promote education change. Among those principles was number 10: Changes that have the support of more than one critical element are most likely to succeed. Compulsory education, with legal, social, and educational support, did not have to overcome as much resistance as it would have encountered had only educators supported it. While this principle is only common sense, it is widely ignored in school reform efforts today.

Of the approximately 750 different questions asked in the first quarter-century of annual PDK/Gallup polls, more than 100 had to do with current experiments or proposed changes in some aspect of U.S. education. "Charting the Changes," the section that concludes this chapter, summarizes the findings from these questions. More than one-third of the questions were asked at least twice, so that opinion trends on several innovations can be traced over varying time spans.

Perhaps the most striking generalization one can draw from this chart is that the public appeared to welcome better than 60% of the changes on which they were questioned. Many of the approved changes are in various stages of adoption in different states and different school districts of the United States. Many are still the subject of debate within the profession and among state and national legislators.

Among the latter are national standards for what children should know and be able to do at various stages of schooling and national tests to assess progress. These are issues on which the public's attitudes have been clear for years, while the profession dithers and finds objections. I do not mean to imply that the objections are merely self-serving. Plainly, the current emphasis on standards-setting and high-stakes assessment, if not accompanied by equally strenuous efforts to support minority students or ensure that new measurements are fair, can be extremely damaging. I suggest only that policy makers must take account of public opinion as they attempt to balance the claims of excellence and the claims of equal opportunity.

The chart of changes invites a number of other generalizations and observations. First of all, there appear to be few common threads among the approved changes beyond the fact that all hold some prospect for school improvement. They cover a wide spectrum of school concerns: curriculum (both expansion and contraction), achievement standards, finance, instructional strategies, parental responsibility, facility use, equalization of opportunity, expansion of school aims and functions, job training and placement, and so on.

No doubt people answered many of these questions without having given them more than a passing thought. Thus the answers usually represent snap judgments, based mainly on generalized attitudes or lifelong prejudices, rather than rational and deliberate consideration of pros and cons. As a matter of fact, respondents usually confess ignorance when pressed to back up their judgments with facts or appeals to authority. And on the more technical questions, the "don't knows" and "no opinions" mount. This is not to denigrate poll findings on such subjects as, say, the adequacy of teacher training. One can have no hope of dealing effectively with opinion without knowing its sources, nature, direction, and intensity; and the polls help us gather this information.

It is interesting to trace the evolution of opinion on such subjects of special concern to parents as lengthening the school year and year-round schooling. The traditional nine-month school year, with vacation coming in the summer, grows out of our agrarian antecedents. It is only in the past decade that a majority of Americans have come to recognize that the factors that gave birth to this traditional calendar are no longer compelling and that new developments such as air conditioning; a complex, technology-driven economy with global competition; and so on, make modifications in this tradition possible and perhaps desirable.

As this chapter was being written, the National Education Commission on Time and Learning, a congressionally mandated group whose members spent two years looking at education in Germany and Japan, issued a report confirming that American high school students spend less than half the time their German, French, and Japanese counterparts spend in the core subjects: their own language, mathematics, and science. American high school students spend an average of 1,460 hours on these subjects compared to 3,525 hours in Germany, for instance.

Unsurprisingly, the commission recommended significant increases in the length of the school day and year, thus abandoning patterns established to accommodate to the needs and rhythms of the farm. Poll respondents, as mentioned previously in this chapter, have begun to agree.

In some cases, poll respondents have told us for years that they approve of certain changes long resisted — often for good reason — by educators. An example is ethical and moral education. Teachers shy away from offering courses in moral/ethical education for a variety of reasons, among which is the fact that consensus on the bases of morality has never been achieved and is unlikely ever to be achieved. The potential for destructive controversy is great. Moreover, the promise of instruction is small. Educators recognize, for example, that morality is more often "caught" than "taught." In any case, educators are likely to ask, isn't morality the responsibility of the family and the church? Yet public opinion favors more attention to ethics and values in the curriculum, as the chart shows.

For educators, sex education is another area of doubt and ambiguity. Although successfully installed in the curriculum of many districts, it is avoided in many more because of real or imagined community opposition. In the poll, sex education was an issue that demanded several probing queries rather than one global question. The 1970 poll asked if people approved or disapproved of schools giving courses in sex education. A 65% to 28% majority did approve. (High school juniors and seniors, asked the same question, were far more enthusiastic, approving by 89% to 8%.)

By 1981, when a sex education question was next asked, poll planners had decided to probe. They discovered that 70% of the public (and 79% of both public school and private school parents) would include sex education in the high school instructional program, but only 45% (and about 55% of parents) approved of it for grades 4 through 8. They also discovered that certain topics in sex education are still taboo for a large number of people. Even among those who approved of sex education in general, bare majorities favored discussion of abortion, homosexuality, and the nature of sexual intercourse as topics for instruction at the high school level. Only a small minority approved these topics for discussion in elementary school. Interestingly enough, birth control was among topics most generally approved for the sex education curriculum, and no significant differences were found among demographic groups, including Protestants and Catholics. Sex education in general, however, was much more likely to win approval from young and better-educated respondents than from older people with no college experience.

By 1987, AIDS education topped the list of topics approved by the public for sex education, as was instruction about other sexually transmitted diseases. Four years later the New York City schools began free distribution of condoms to high school students, primarily as an AIDS control measure. Several other large cities followed suit, including Los Angeles, San Francisco, and Seattle. To the surprise of many observers, the 1992 poll revealed that 68% of the public approved of free condom distribution in the high schools. However, for nearly half of these, approval was contingent on parent permission, a reservation that almost certainly would vitiate effectiveness of the program. And when the question was asked again the next year, many people apparently had second thoughts; the approval total dropped to 60%.

Demographic differences in the public's reaction to such issues as sex education and condom distribution illustrate particularly well the value of local or regional polls when policy decisions are contemplated. There were striking differences in the attitudes of rural and small-town respondents compared to urban communities, and equally pronounced differences between the South and the West.

Performance contracting attracted a nod of approval from 49% of respondents to the 1971 Gallup poll before that fad sank into oblivion. The Nineties equivalent of that Seventies phenomenon is the current privatization movement, manifested in such disparate for-profit enterprises as the Celebration School and Teaching Academy now being built just outside of Orlando, Florida, by the Walt Disney Company; the Whittle Schools, popularly known as the Edison Project; and Education Alternatives Incorporated (EAI) of Minneapolis, which is in the second year of a five-year, $133 million contract to run nine Baltimore schools and is seeking major contracts in Hartford, Connecticut, Washington, D.C., and elsewhere.

So far there are only a few companies in the field, compared with hundreds in the heyday of performance contracting, but already Whittle is in trouble. And EAI, while proving it can repair broken windows quickly in Baltimore, has a lot to prove in the classrooms. Its so-called Testeract Way teaching strategy is essentially a collection of reforms already introduced in public education: hands-on science and math, group learning and team teaching, mainstreaming special education students, individualized education plans, and well-supplied classrooms. EAI risks slipping on the same banana peel that upset Dorsett: teaching to the test. Using computer drills (Dorsett used relatively primitive teaching machines), EAI concentrates on raising students' scores on the standardized basic skills tests used in Maryland.

Although scaled down from the ambitious original program envisaged by Chris Whittle, the Edison Project still talks of opening 10 to 15 elementary schools, to enroll 10,000 students, in the fall of 1995. Its lofty goals — students speaking two languages by the end of fifth grade and passing six advanced placement exams before graduating — would require a longer school day and year and a host of other reforms. The Edison Project's financial future is insecure, with the parent company likely to have lost $30 million in 1994. It remains to be seen if 70% of the nation's school systems could be run at a profit, as the company's computer model projects. A 1994 *U.S. News and World Report* article warned that "it's a long way from a computer model to money in the bank" ("Selling the Schools: Is Private Enterprise the Future of Public Education in America?" *U.S. News and World Report*, 7 May 1994.)

The 1994 PDK/Gallup poll showed even less support for privatization (45% for, 47% against) than the 1971 poll did for performance contracting (49% for, 28% against).

In summary, it can be said that the American public is almost universally supportive of changes that hold even faint promise of improving the public schools' capacity to meet sound education goals. But people are not ready to embrace changes that might threaten the principles on which public education is grounded. Thus they are wary of wholesale privatization or vouchers that have the potential for weakening public schools and creating a two-tiered, elitist system. In short, the public would extract the best from both the liberal and the conservative traditions in American thought.

Charting the Changes

Change Considered	Year	Favor %	Oppose %
Parents take more active part in educating their children	1993	96	3
More career education	1973	90	7
	1976	80	5
Improve quality of schooling in poorer states and communities	1989	83	9
	1993	90	8
Make financial support for girls' athletics equal to boys	1974	88	7
Keep school buildings open after school hours during vacations	1992	87	-
. . . during weekends		67	-
. . . during holidays		72	-
High school credit for community service	1978	87	8
	1984	79	16
. . . as a graduation requirement	1989	61	30
	1993	70	29
Work-study programs for students not interested in school	1974	86	9
Public school job training for 15- to 18-year-old unemployed dropouts	1975	86	11
Make parents financially responsible for vandalism in school by their child(ren)	1978	86	11
Make school personnel available for counseling with single parents in evening	1980	86	10
State board exams for teacher certification	1979	85	9
	1981	84	11
	1984	89	7
	1986	85	11
Periodic testing for teachers to retain certification	1979	85	10
	1988	86	11
National standards for teacher certification	1988	86	9
Test school principals periodically	1979	85	10
Allocate same amount of money per student even if takes from wealthy districts	1993	85	12
Parents confer with school personnel at start of each semester	1980	84	11
Compulsory programs on effects of drugs and alcohol	1975	84	11

33

Change Considered	Year	Favor %	Oppose %
Fund-raising for projects, equipment by teachers and students	1971	84	11
Settle teacher strikes by arbitration	1975	84	7
	1982	79	7
More state, federal assistance for students to attend college	1989	83	13
Special classes to teach English to immigrants	1980	82	13
Computers for instruction	1983	81	10
National tests to compare academic achievement among schools	1970	75	16
	1971	70	21
	1983	75	17
	1986	77	16
	1988	81	14
Required national achievement standards and goals	1989	70	19
	1991	81	12
Kindergarten as part of public schools	1986	80	13
. . . as compulsory part public schools	1986	71	22
Standardized national tests for high school graduation	1976	65	31
	1981	69	26
	1984	65	29
	1988	73	22
More emphasis on certain high school subjects			
Math	1990	80	
English		79	
Computers		79	
Careers		73	
Science		68	
Moral/ethical education*	1975	79	15
	1980	79	16
	1981	70	17
Constitutional amendment to permit prayer in public schools	1974	77	17
	1987	68	26
Early high school graduation if meet academic requirements	1977	74	22
	1980	77	19
Use school facilities for delivery of health and social services	1992	77	16

*In 1987 a majority said they thought it possible to develop courses on character education that would be acceptable to the people of their communities.

Change Considered	Year	Favor %	Oppose %
High school credit for volunteer work by students not interested in school	1974	77	17
Improve standards to improve schools	1987	76	11
Stricter standards for high school graduation	1986	70	24
Activities at school for latch-key kids	1980	76	18
Grade promotion only if students can pass test	1978	68	27
	1983	75	20
Restrict class size to as few as 15 in early grades*	1989	75	18
Sex education	1970	65	28
. . . in high school	1981	70	22
. . . in elementary school	1981	45	48
. . . in high school	1985	75	19
. . . in elementary school	1985	52	43
. . . in high school	1987	76	16
. . . in elementary school	1987	55	37
Prohibition of smoking by students on school property	1981	71	25
Achievement standards for grade promotion should be more strict	1986	72	22
Nongraded (continuous progress) schools	1972	71	22
	1975	64	28
	1980	62	30
More effort to promote racial toleration, understanding	1992	71	16
More after-school and summer programs for children whose parents work	1989	71	21
Standardized, imposed national curriculum	1989	69	21
	1991	68	24
National youth service and training for unemployed males under 18	1979	67	27
. . . for females		62	31
More authority for local school boards, less for state and federal governments	1977	67	25
Constitutional amendment to equalize per-pupil spending	1974	66	22
Standardized national test for high school graduation**	1976	65	31
	1980	69	26

---

*68% willing to pay more taxes for this purpose; 25% opposed.

**Gallup first asked this question in 1958, before the Gallup/PDK polls were started. In that year 50% approved, 39% disapproved.

Change Considered	Year	Favor %	Oppose %
Job placement by schools for recent graduates	1980	64	30
Give principals more authority	1989	63	26
Permit schools to collect personal information helpful for counseling, individualizing	1990	60	32
Alternative schools	1973	62	26
Parental choice among public schools	1989	60	31
	1990	62	31
	1991	62	33
	1993	65	33
Deny driver's license to dropouts	1991	62	32
Allow girls to participate in non-contact sports with boys	1974	59	35
Low-interest loans to all college students	1981	59	36
Tax-supported public school child-care centers for preschoolers	1976	46	49
	1981	46	47
	1985	43	45
	1993	59	38
Fundamental (back-to-basics) schools	1977	34*	5*
Schools without walls	1972	56	34
Year of internship for teachers at half pay before certification	1980	56	36
Lengthen school year by 30 days	1982	37	53
	1983	40	49
	1984	44	50
	1991	51	42
	1992	55	35
	1993**	52	47
Charter schools	1994	54	39
Mainstream the physically handicapped	1979	53	36
Mainstream the mentally handicapped	1979	13	77
	1992	22	67
Year-round school	1970	42	49
	1988	40	53

*Only 41% of 1977 poll respondents had heard the term "back-to-basics." Of these, 83% approved of the concept and 11% disapproved, resulting in these low percentages.

**Q. Do you favor or oppose increasing the amount of time students spend in the public schools in your community?

Change Considered	Year	Favor %	Oppose %
Constitutional amendment to permit some government financial aid to parochial schools	1974	52	35
Extend scope of negotiations beyond wages and hours	1976	52	39
Volunteers to direct extracurricular activities, coach	1981	52	41
Spend more for instruction of students with learning problems than for average students	1982	42	52
	1985	51	42
	1988	48	47
Parental fines for child's frequent truancy	1977	51	40
Higher pay for math, science teachers than for others	1983	50	35
Voucher system	1970	43	46
	1971	38	44
	1981	43	41
	1983	51	38
	1985	45	40
	1986	46	41
	1987	44	41
	1991	50	39
Performance contracting (private company guarantees certain level of achievement)	1971	49	28
Some tax money to help parochial schools	1970	48	44
	1981	40	51
	1986	42	50
Tax money to help private schools	1986	27	65
Contract with private, profit-making corporations to run some schools	1994	45	47
Preschool child care as part of public school system	1976	46	49
	1981	46	47
Permit public school teacher strikes	1969	37	59
	1975	45	48
	1980	40	52
	1981	37	56
Lengthen school day by one hour	1982	37	55
	1983	41	48
Live-in boarding schools at public expense for children unable to function in regular schools	1976	39	50
Schools do more to promote racial integration	1973	30	61
	1988	37	54

Change Considered	Year	Favor %	Oppose %
Make attendance optional for longer day or year	1991	36	56
Allow advertising in return for free equipment and news program	1994	38	57
Change curriculum to meet today's needs	1970	31	46
	1982	36	42
Value-added tax (national sales tax) to reduce property tax	1972	35	51
Schools arrange schedule so children get home at same time as working parents	1977	33	59
Start school at age 4	1972	32	64
	1973	30	64
	1986	29	64
Conduct vocational education outside the public school system	1978	32	53
More independent study	1971	31	47
Permit school-leaving at age 14 if pass minimum tests	1976	30	66
Home schooling	1985	16	73
	1988	28	59
Four-year colleges/universities raise entrance requirements	1984	27	59
Parental choice of private school at public expense	1993	24	74
Dismissal for frequent absenteeism	1978	19	63*
Constitutional amendment to prohibit forced busing for integration	1974	18	72
Federal government pay all costs of college education	1969	16	81
Open schools	1975	13**	10**

*Percent favoring "forced" attendance.

**60% of respondents didn't know what was meant by term.

CHAPTER 4

MAJOR PUBLIC
SCHOOL PROBLEMS

"What do you think are the biggest problems with which the public schools in this community must deal?"

That is the first education question Phi Delta Kappa/Gallup poll respondents hear after they agree to an interview and get the demographics* out of the way. It is also the only question that has been asked in every one of the PDK/Gallup surveys taken to date.

It is difficult to tabulate answers to any open-ended question and particularly this one. With some open-ended questions, "miscellaneous" turns out to be the largest response category; but in this case that problem has been avoided. The miscellaneous category for this question seldom has totaled 5% and usually is much smaller than the "don't know" category, which once reached 16%. ("There are no problems" is offered by 3% to 5% of respondents.)

Squeezing the responses into the 50 or so categories developed over the years is difficult. For example, some problems never have gained more than a 3% response, including mismanagement of funds/programs, communication problems, problems with administration, school board policies, transportation, non-English-speaking students, government interference, teacher strikes, moral standards, declining enrollments, school board politics, lack of after-school programs, dropouts, lack of family structure, lack of good or up-to-date equipment, taxes too high, too much emphasis on sports, peer pressure, and sex/pregnancy. But they are nonetheless real problems.

The question is asked every year for several good reasons. First, a respondent's true feelings tend to leap out, uncontaminated by the

---

*Demographics include sex, race, age, education and income levels, occupation, religion, preferred political party, number of children in public and private schools, and other factors that make it possible to discern differences in opinion among respondent subgroups.

views or preconceived categories in the minds of people who devise poll questions. Are the answers uninformed? Often. Superficial? Sometimes. Unsophisticated? Of course. But in aggregate, these opinions shape the reality with which school authorities must deal. They tell us what is genuinely bothering people about their schools. And often they reveal misconceptions that the education profession should try to rectify.

Three problem categories have dominated the list for the past quarter-century. They are "discipline," mentioned most frequently in 16 of the first 17 years; "drugs," named most frequently in six of the last nine years; and "finance," first in 1993, tied for first in 1992, and first in 1971. Discipline has never been lower than third in the list. Drugs first appeared in the list in 1970 (as number 6 in mentions); after 1978, drugs as a problem for schools was never lower than third. Finance has ranked among the top four problems in 25 of 26 years.

Following are other perennial problems noted by respondents:

- "Integration/segregation" became "integration/busing" after 1975, when people began increasingly to question the wisdom of court-ordered busing to integrate the races in the public schools.
- "Difficulty of getting good teachers" is a major concern for many people. Had it been combined with "teachers' lack of interest or ability," this category would often have ranked third or fourth, after discipline, drugs, and finance.
- "Curriculum" (or better, "poor curriculum") was mentioned by only a small minority of respondents — 4% to 7% — until 1977, when 10% of respondents thought of it as a major problem. After 1978 the category became "curriculum/standards" so as to take into account the perception held by many people that school achievement standards were declining. From that year through 1993, it was never lower than fifth in the problems list and was mentioned by from 8% to 15% of all poll respondents.

In most of the recent poll reports that have appeared in the *Phi Delta Kappan*, problems mentioned by 2% or fewer respondents have been omitted. As noted, the full list of categories built over the years now exceeds 50. Several of these categories can be considered "problems of the local schools" only by a stretch of logic or definition. For example, in the very first poll some form of "using new, up-to-date methods" was apparently considered a problem by 15 or more of the respondents. In 1978, "parents' involvement in school activities" — usually considered a plus by students of education — was mentioned as a problem by several respondents. ("Meddling in school business" might have offered a better pigeon-hole for this problem.)

Obviously, many of the categories used in poll reports are related. For example, "lack of proper finances" may well account for "lack of proper facilities," "low teacher pay," and "large schools/overcrowding." And a dissertation could be written — may already have been written — about the relationship between "lack of respect for teachers" and "difficulty of getting good teachers." "Pupils' lack of interest/truancy" may well grow out of "poor curriculum"; at the very least, an inadequate curriculum exacerbates lack of interest.

It is clear that poll respondents seldom made a distinction between problems that are susceptible of solution or amelioration through programs that schools can initiate and problems inherent in the larger society, many of which may be well beyond the effective reach of the public schools. However, when people were asked to make this distinction, as they were in some of the polls, they proved capable of doing so.

The Meaning of Discipline

In public perceptions over the past quarter-century, "poor discipline" or "lack of proper discipline" has always ranked among the greatest problems facing the public schools. As many as one-fourth of PDK/Gallup poll respondents have mentioned it in a given year. Had there been a Gallup survey on school problems when America shook off British rule more than two centuries ago, I do not doubt that bad behavior in school would have topped the list even then. The problem is as old as civilization.

There is no dearth of advice on how to deal with adult-disapproved behavior in the classroom and school yard. Education theory and research — drawing on the various schools of thought, philosophy, and psychology — have provided teachers with a panoply of sometimes conflicting principles and practices. While disdaining "discipline" as a discipline, teacher preparatory institutions have grudgingly built units of instruction and practice around the discipline problem. Yet no satisfying consensus has emerged on such topics as corporal punishment (prohibited in only a handful of U.S. states), suspension and expulsion, and the agonizing puzzle of incorrigible juvenile delinquency. Today, in fact, Americans are stunned by increasingly violent behavior among the young, whose worst offenses only a generation ago we recall as chewing gum and whispering in class. Violence emerged in the 1994

41

poll in a virtual tie with discipline as the number-one problem of public schools as viewed by the public.

When school discipline popped up in the early PDK/Gallup polls as a major public concern, poll planners determined to explore public perceptions of poor discipline: the behavior that reveals it, its putative causes, suggestions for amelioration, and locus of responsibility for improvement. In the 1973 poll this question was asked: "When we talk about 'discipline' in the schools, just what does this mean to you?" (The question was repeated in 1982.)

In reporting the 1973 poll, George Gallup noted that most respondents saw discipline as a matter of obeying rules; respecting views of parents, teachers, and others in authority; and being considerate of fellow students who wish to learn in a peaceful atmosphere. These typical responses show the range of reactions:

> "Discipline is self-control and proper respect for other students and for those in authority."
> "Without discipline, neither school nor society could exist. The world would be bedlam."
> "Where learning takes place without confusion."
> "Proper discipline makes children happier. When they run wild, they are undone by the confusion they create."
> "Discipline is respect for the teacher on the part of the child and respect for the child on the part of the teacher."

Gallup suggested in his report that, "while law and order have become almost code words for the conservative viewpoint in politics, the basic concept is held in high regard by the public. In fact, in the 1972 survey, when asked to choose from a list of nine goals of education, the public placed 'teaching students to respect law and authority' as the top goal for students in grades 7-12."

In 1982, Gallup reported responses to the "meaning of discipline" question under six substantive headings: obeying rules/regulations (mentioned by 54% of respondents), authority/control by teachers (31%), respect for teachers (18%), students' lack of willingness to learn (7%), fighting/violence (3%), smoking/drugs (2%).

How closely do the breaches of proper discipline that the public perceives match the breaches perceived by teachers? Do teachers and the public agree on the seriousness of the discipline problem in the public schools? We have fairly recent answers to all of these questions from the PDK/Gallup public poll and two others conducted among teachers, commissioned by Phi Delta Kappa and conducted by the Gallup Organization in 1984 and 1989.

The question was stated: "How serious a problem would you say discipline is in the public schools of your community — very serious, fairly serious, not too serious, or not at all serious?" Table 5 compares public and teacher responses.

Table 5. Seriousness of discipline problem.

	U.S. Public 1984 %	All Teachers 1984 %	All Teachers 1989 %
Very serious	34	16	11
Fairly serious	24	33	39
Not too serious	32	35	42
Not at all serious	4	14	8
No opinion	6	2	-

Teacher and public respondents also were asked to estimate the frequency of 18 different kinds of student discipline problems that were commonly reported. The question was asked in the following forms:

Of the public: "As I read off the following problems by letter, would you please tell me how often you think each problem occurs in the public schools in this community — just your impression?"

Of teachers: "About how often do each of the problems listed occur at the school in which you teach?"

Table 6 compares these responses. This table invites several observations. First, almost all of the 18 listed behaviors fall within the public's definition of discipline problems. A possible exception is the behavior that both teachers and the public saw as the most common problem of all: school work and homework assignments not completed.

Second, teachers identified "behavior that disrupts class" as a very or fairly frequent problem, worse in 1989 than in 1984. (Most of the other 1984 to 1989 differences in teacher responses could be accounted for by sampling error.) The public saw disruptive classroom behavior as being only slightly more common than did teachers.

Third, and perhaps most important, in 17 of 18 cases the public perceived these undesirable behaviors as being considerably more frequent than did teachers. No one can deny that teachers are in a better position than the public to know the facts of the matter. Here again, the best

Table 6. Frequency of discipline problems.

	Most of the Time/Fairly Often*						
	All Teachers		**Elementary Teachers**		**High School Teachers**		**U.S. Public**
	1984 %	1989 %	1984 %	1989 %	1984 %	1989 %	1984 %
School work and homework assignments not completed	76	79	73	76	80	85	64
Behavior that disrupts class	47	57	48	60	47	50	60
Truancy/being absent from school	47	45	29	32	62	67	53
Talking back to, disobeying teachers	43	45	42	45	43	44	56
Cheating on tests	40	45	29	33	51	64	46
Sloppy or inappropriate dress	37	45	33	43	41	49	47
Skipping classes	35	29	16	18	57	59	56
Stealing money or personal property belonging to other students, teachers, or staff	32	32	25	26	39	40	38
Vandalizing of school property	29	25	22	20	35	34	39
Theft of school property	23	15	18	13	29	19	34
Use of drugs at school	17	14	6	5	29	30	53
Selling drugs at school	13	14	4	1	24	32	47
Drinking alcoholic beverages at school	10	6	2	1	17	14	35
Carrying of knives, firearms, or other weapons at school	8	4	5	3	10	8	29
Sexual activity at school	8	6	3	1	12	13	24
Racial fights between whites, blacks, Hispanics, or other minorities	4	6	3	5	5	9	22
Taking money or property by force, using weapons or threats	2	2	2	2	2	2	18
Physical attacks on teachers or staff	1	2	1	2	1	2	15

(Figures add to more than 100% because of multiple answers.)

*Because of significant differences in responses from teachers by level taught, the table provides figures for both high school and elementary teachers.

explanation one can offer for the manifest difference is the fact that a large majority of lay respondents — more than 65% — were getting their information about the schools secondhand, generally from the media, and so received a distorted view of what goes on in the schools.

Students themselves, surveyed in a study commissioned by Phi Delta Kappa in 1986, agree with teachers that discipline is not as serious a problem, or as general a problem, as the public believes. Lack of discipline was mentioned by only 8% of high school seniors surveyed, whereas in the PDK/Gallup poll that year, 24% of the adult respondents considered it a major problem. It is also worth noting that 17.2% of the 1986 high school seniors viewed school disciplinary rules as too strict. A full 50% of the general public, in the three years (1969-1971) when the question was asked by the Gallup Organization, said discipline was not strict enough in their local schools; only 2% thought it too strict. Obviously, perceptions follow angle of view.

Causes and Cures of Discipline Problems

The PDK/Gallup polls explored the public's views regarding the causes of discipline problems only once, in the 1983 poll; but it is unlikely that opinions have changed much since. The question was phrased in this way: "Many people say that discipline is one of the major problems of the public schools today. Would you please look over this list and tell me which reasons you think are most important to explain why there is a discipline problem?" Table 7 records the responses.

Table 7. Causes of discipline problems.

	Percent
Lack of discipline in the home	72
Lack of respect for law and authority throughout society	54
Students who are constant troublemakers often can't be removed from school	42
Some teachers are not properly trained to deal with discipline problems	42
The courts have made school administrators so cautious that they don't deal severely with student misbehavior	41
Viewing television programs that emphasize crime and violence	39
Punishment is too lenient	39
Decline in the teaching of good manners	37
Teachers themselves do not command respect	36
Failure on the part of teachers to make classroom work more interesting	31
One-parent families	26

If lack of discipline begins in the home, as the vast majority of poll respondents believe, does it follow that correction should begin there as well? Evidence that people recognize the logic of this proposition appeared in responses to a 1985 poll question on solutions to the discipline problem.

In that year, a large majority liked the idea of setting up discussion groups and required classes for parents of problem children. They also voted for special classes for teachers on how to deal with these troublesome and often troubled students. Suspension of students with extreme behavior problems gained considerably less approval, as did other harsh measures. This comes as something of a surprise, when one considers the public's strong law-and-order bent. On two occasions (1970 and 1988) poll respondents approved of corporal punishment, although the margin of approval diminished in the later poll. Approval was much less general in 1988 than in 1970. Interestingly enough, a higher percentage of teachers (56%) than of lay persons (50%) favored spanking and other forms of physical punishment when asked the question in 1989.

The 1974 poll asked what should be done with a high school student who refuses to obey his teachers. A majority of the public poll respondents chose punitive action: suspension/expulsion, 31%; punishment (nature unspecified), 11%; paddling, 7%; and detention time, 4%. A large group chose "rehabilitative" measures: involving parents, 22%; counseling, 13%; provision of special curricula and teachers, 10%; discussion with the principal, teachers, and juvenile authorities, 8%; and miscellaneous other ameliorative programs, including work/study.

In 1975 the Supreme Court handed down two decisions (*Goss* v. *Lopez* and *Wood* v. *Strickland*) requiring school authorities to provide full due process in disciplinary cases involving students. Of respondents who were aware of the decision (41% of the total), about one-fourth thought the court went too far in making the ruling. Another 1975 poll question found that nearly five times as many people believed that public school students had too many rights and privileges as believed they had too few.

In related questions asked in 1975, these opinions came to light:

- If special public schools with strict discipline, including a dress code and emphasis on the three R's, were available, 57% of respondents would enroll their children in them. Only 33% said no, they would not.

- Respondents believed, by a large margin, that students in both elementary and high school were not made to work as hard as they should.

How strongly the public feels about parental responsibility for student behavior was revealed in responses to a question asked in the 1978 poll. An overwhelming 86% of respondents said parents should be made financially responsible for damage to school property done by their children; only 11% thought otherwise.

Another indicator of the depth of public conviction about the importance of school discipline lies in the answer to a question on school choice, asked in 1991. Firm, well-maintained student discipline ranked number two in importance among 12 factors people would consider in choosing a school for their child, given free choice. People also rated firm discipline first among strategies for helping low-income and racial or ethnic minority students to succeed in school.

Answers to still other poll questions are relevant to the discipline problem. For example, the public is willing to grant school authorities great latitude in searching student lockers for stolen items or illicit drugs. And in reacting to the six national education goals announced by President Bush and the state governors in 1990, the public chose goal six, "a disciplined environment, free of drugs and violence," as most important.

In short, the public is consistent in the beliefs 1) that students in U.S. public schools lack proper discipline and 2) that improved discipline is the answer to many of the schools' other problems.

Parents and the schools should deal with most of the serious breaches of behavioral codes in school, the public said in the 1980 survey. However, a plurality thought the courts should have major responsibility for dealing with vandalism of school property or bringing weapons to school. Although Table 8 obscures the combination, in fact, a substantial portion of respondents believed, in 1980, that most of these problems should be dealt with by school authorities *and* parents, with resort to the courts only in extreme cases.

Truancy, the public believes, is the only behavior problem that is primarily a parental responsibility. The question was: "Here are some student behavior problems which may occur in school. In your opinion, who should deal with each kind of problem — should it be the parents, the school, or the courts?" Table 8 shows the responses.

Table 8. Who should deal with discipline problems.

	*Parents %	School %	Courts %	Don't Know %
Truancy (skipping school)	72	45	9	2
Vandalism of school property	44	39	50	2
Bringing weapons to school	41	35	59	3
Fighting in school	42	75	10	3
Using alcohol or drugs on school property	50	57	35	2
Striking a teacher	43	56	35	3
Stealing money or clothing from other students	48	58	30	3

*Multiple answers permitted.

The Problem of Drugs

In recent years, drug abuse is the most commonly mentioned major problem of "the public schools of this community." It is significant that the national goal that "every school in America will be free of drugs and violence and will offer a disciplined environment conducive to learning" received the highest priority rating of any of the national goals in the two PDK/Gallup polls that have asked for ratings. In 1990, 55% of respondents gave it a "very high" priority and three years later elevated that figure to 71%. No other goal came close, though all were rated "very high" by at least 40% of the respondents.

However, people are not at all confident that the goal can be reached. In fact, when asked in the 1990 poll, 36% said it was very unlikely that it would be. This was the highest "unlikely" rating given to any of the goals; even the goal of being first in the world in science and math achievement was considered by fewer respondents (24%) to be very unlikely of attainment.

People appear to understand some of the limitations facing school efforts to control drug abuse among the young. In the 1988 poll they expressed relatively low confidence in the ability of the public schools to deal with drug abuse. In fact, only 9% said they had a great deal of confidence in the schools' ability to deal with the problem, 37% said a "fair amount," and 35% said "not very much." Twelve percent expressed no confidence at all.

Another indicator that people understand that the schools' role in combating drug abuse among the young may not be crucial lies in findings from the 1989 poll. Respondents were asked to rank the potency of various educational influences on children. They considered the student's family most influential (63% response), the school second (47%), the student's peers third (41%), and television fourth (32%).

Nevertheless, Americans want it all. They would have the schools place more emphasis on drug education and training while cutting "frills" in the curriculum and returning to basics. But only reluctantly would they lengthen the school day or year in such a way as to accommodate all of the demands.

In 1975, for example, 84% of respondents said yes (and only 11% no) to the question: Should the schools of this country require students to attend a program on the effects of drugs and alcohol? In 1990 the percentage jumped to 90%, having risen from 81% in 1983 and 82% in 1984. It was the highest percentage given to any in a list of fringe subjects, including (in order) alcohol abuse education, AIDS education, sex education, environmental issues and problems, teen pregnancy, driver education, character education, parenting/parent training, dangers of nuclear waste, dangers of nuclear war, and communism/socialism.

Some observers have speculated that the recent upturn in drug use and cigarette smoking among high school students may be related to increased emphasis on the "challenging" subject matter of national goal number six: English, mathematics, science, history, and geography — which has necessarily been accompanied by de-emphasis on such subjects as health education. They also suggest that increased drug use may be a form of escapism from the new pressure for excellence in the challenging subjects. Finally, there is a question as to whether renewed dropout prevention efforts may inflate drug use figures, as in the past drug users were more likely to drop out of school than they now are.

It is important to distinguish between two major categories of problems that affect the ability of the schools to achieve the goals they have been assigned or have accepted. First, there are problems that arise in the larger society because of influences and developments not directly related to formal schooling. Drug abuse is one of these. No one has ever seriously blamed the schools for drug abuse. Then there are problems that arise because of deficiencies or failures to adapt in school curriculum, facilities, teaching methods, or program scope. To choose but one such deficiency, consider widespread ignorance of geography among high school graduates. It seems fair to assign some blame to schools for that kind of ignorance.

49

In general, people have made the distinction between these two types of problem, either consciously or subconsciously. Answers to a poll question asked in 1990 seem to confirm such a generalization. The question was asked: "In your opinion, which is more at fault for most of the problems facing public education in this community — the performance of the local public schools or the effect of societal problems?" Overwhelmingly, with percentages among subgroups ranging from 63% to 75%, the response was "the effect of societal problems."

But these findings do not mean that public schools can ignore most societal problems and concentrate their efforts on limited academic objectives. Societal problems impinge on, limit, skew, and truncate those efforts. Thus drug abuse is a societal problem whose manifestations in the school must be dealt with in the school. To whatever extent is feasible, the school's mission must be to address this societal problem.

CHAPTER 5

VOUCHERS AND CHOICE

The Struggle for the Soul of American Education: That is the portentous subtitle of Peter Cookson's brilliant new book, *School Choice* (1994). This work is probably the most comprehensive and objective treatment of the topic yet to be published. Cookson risked sounding over-dramatic because he is convinced of the overwhelming significance of this issue for America's education future. Other leading education theorists and historians would agree.

Henry Levin (1990), for example, believes that the debate raging over choice will test a basic tenet of democracy. He says:

> Education lies at the intersection of two sets of competing rights. The first is the right of parents to choose the experiences, influences, and values to which they expose their children, i.e., the right to raise their children as they see fit. The second is the right of a democratic society to use the educational system as a means to reproduce its most essential political, economic, and social institutions through a common schooling experience.

Levin concludes that the only way to promote cohesion and tolerance in society is to give people this common schooling experience, which is threatened by some choice plans — certainly those involving vouchers redeemable at nonpublic schools.

Cookson reflects Levin's concerns when he says, "A strong public school system is the nursery of democracy," but he also professes to believe that "choice can be a mechanism for producing a system that is just, innovative, and academically productive. It is a method by which we can reinvent public education, reintegrate schools into their communities, and redefine community." Is this possible?

The Phi Delta Kappa/Gallup polls have repeatedly examined public opinion on voucher and parental choice issues. Attitudes toward vouchers were first surveyed, at the insistence of George Gallup, Sr., in the

51

second poll of the series, taken in 1970, at a time when there was little activity related to vouchers on the state legislative front. The only national figure promoting the voucher idea at that time was Milton Friedman, who later received the Nobel Prize in economics in 1976.

But "innovation" was a watchword of ambitious educators in the early Seventies. Performance contracting attracted 100 different organizations to enter into contracts worth an estimated $200 million; the first results of the National Assessment of Educational Progress were unveiled; the first National Conference on Environmental Education was held, following the first observance of Earth Day. It was not long before school choice and vouchers came under discussion.

Several questions on change were asked in this same 1970 poll, with these results: Nearly one-third (31%) of the respondents thought the local schools' curriculum was in need of change to meet the day's needs. Twenty percent thought their local schools were not sufficiently interested in trying new ideas (although 21% thought them too ready). And nearly half of the respondents (48%) favored the use of tax money to help parochial schools "make ends meet," while 44% said no and 8% had no opinion. This was the high-water mark for public approval of "parochiaid," as it was then called. In 1981, when the same question was next asked, support had dropped to 40% and opposition had risen to 51%; there was no significant change in these percentages five years later.

The voucher question was asked in 1970 in this way: "In some nations, the government allots a certain amount of money for each child's education. The parents can then send the child to any public, parochial, or private school they choose. This is called the 'voucher system.' Would you like to see such an idea adopted in this country?" Table 9 shows eight years of responses.

Table 9. Approve or disapprove a 'voucher system.'

	National Totals							
	1991 %	1987 %	1986 %	1985 %	1983 %	1981 %	1971 %	1970 %
Favor	50	44	46	45	51	43	38	43
Oppose	39	41	41	40	38	41	44	46
Don't know	11	15	13	15	11	16	18	11

The 1987 poll followed the voucher question with another asking whether people thought the voucher system would help or hurt the local public schools. Forty-two percent said they thought vouchers would hurt the public schools, and 36% said they thought vouchers would help. Of those who *favored* vouchers, 73% thought vouchers would help the local public schools; of those *opposed* to vouchers, 81% thought that vouchers would damage the local public schools.

Opinion on vouchers was divided rather evenly in all but a couple of years over a 21-year period. Fluctuations of a few percentage points are not evidence of significant shifts in public opinion. The relatively large "don't know" response each year suggests that many people have given little thought to the issue.

What the table does *not* show is a trend toward greater approval of vouchers. *There has been no such trend.* The 50% favorable response in 1991 was matched in 1983 (the year of greatest dissatisfaction with the nation's public schools in the era covered by these polls, and not coincidentally the year of that dissatisfaction-inflating report, *A Nation at Risk*).

After 1991, poll planners decided against using the 1970 voucher question because of a growing conviction that the wording was outmoded; the reference to voucher use in other nations seemed to date and perhaps to bias it. Also, it did not make clear that voucher money is of necessity taxpayer money. Finally, interest had shifted from vouchers to intradistrict and interdistrict choice among public schools, after Minnesota's adoption of the first statewide plan in 1988, followed by Iowa, Arkansas, Ohio, and Nebraska in 1989.

Although Phi Delta Kappa dropped the voucher question, the National Catholic Education Association picked it up, word for word, in a 1993 survey. This survey, also conducted by the Gallup Organization, obtained a startlingly different reaction. Seventy percent of the respondents reportedly favored vouchers, versus only 27% opposed. How can this sudden apparent shift be explained? Some observers would cite the Bush Administration's decision to back government vouchers for non-public school attendance, a position taken in 1991. But Alec Gallup does not believe that any shift in opinion on the issue has actually occurred. Interviewed in June of 1994, he said:

> Our Lincoln [Nebraska] office conducted this NCEA poll without consulting me. And they made every mistake in the book. The worst was revealing the self-interest of the sponsoring organization in the question schedule that led up to the voucher question.

The NCEA has long hoped for public money for the financially strapped Catholic school system. So poll context accounts largely for what is called, in polling parlance, 'acquiescence': People tend to give you the answer they think you want.

Ideally, we would devote several questions to vouchers/choice in every Phi Delta Kappa poll to be sure we are assessing people's true feelings. Time doesn't always permit it. But we have asked a series of questions in two PDK polls since 1991, and I think we got the basic question right in the 1994 poll. It is stated thus: 'A proposal has been made which would allow parents to send their school-age children to any public, private, or church-related school they choose. For parents choosing nonpublic schools, the government would pay all or part of the tuition. Would you favor or oppose this proposal in your state?'

On this question the division was 45% for and 54% against, with only 1% holding no opinion. I believe these percentages are an accurate reflection of sentiment, at this point in time, and I believe most people have pretty well made up their minds on the issue. The fact that so few were undecided in this poll is consistent with this conviction. Also, the findings are confirmed by the anti-voucher votes in Oregon, Colorado, and California in recent years.

Question wording is crucial, of course; we would probably have found even more than 54% opposition if we had said "government tax money' or 'taxpayer's money' would be used to pay tuition instead of 'government would pay.' I am at last satisfied with question wording. If we use the question again next year, I predict that we will get a 45-55 split again, or very near it.

A 54% opposition to the voucher principle recorded in the 1994 PDK/Gallup poll conceals support among certain demographic groups. Breakdowns by various categories of respondents reveal that Hispanics and Catholics (overlapping categories) and nonpublic school parents (also overlapping) favored tuition vouchers redeemable at nonpublic schools by sizable majorities. The approval margins were 60-40 for Hispanics, 55-44 for Catholics, and 69-29 for nonpublic school parents. However, Hispanics represented only about 5% of all respondents, Catholics 24%, and nonpublic school parents 5%. Demographic groups favoring vouchers by lesser margins were 18- to 29-year-olds (50% for, 49% against), people who did not finish high school (53% for, 40% against), and people with two or more children (51% for, 49% against).

People with no children in school, who made up 52% of the sample, opposed vouchers 57% to 42%. Public schools parents, who constituted 41% of the sample, opposed them by a 51% to 48% margin.

If Not Vouchers, What About Choice?

The 1993 PDK/Gallup poll repeated four questions on *public school* choice and *private school* choice asked in previous polls, but no trends appeared. If anything, people in 1993 were even more adamantly opposed than past respondents to the idea of paying the tuition of non-public school students with public money. But they were in favor — increasingly over the 1989-1993 period — of public school choice.

The most enduring of these four questions, asked in four different years, was: Do you favor or oppose allowing students and their parents to choose which *public* schools in this community the students attend, regardless of where they live? Table 10 shows the results for 1989, 1990, 1991, and 1993.

Table 10. Approve or disapprove public school choice.

	National Totals			
	1993 %	1991 %	1990 %	1989 %
Favor	65	62	62	60
Oppose	33	33	31	31
Don't know	2	5	7	9

The PDK/Gallup polls began probing the sensitive issue of parental choice of *public* schools in 1979. In that year parents were asked if they would like to send their oldest child to a public school different from that currently attended. The great majority (78%) of parents whose oldest child was 12 or younger said no; only 12% said yes. An even larger majority (86%) of parents whose oldest child was older than 12 said no, while 11% said yes. This was hardly a resounding endorsement of public school choice.

However, in 1986 two related questions were asked, with considerably different results. In that year 68% of public school parents said they wished they had the *right* to choose the public schools their children would attend, while 25% said they did not wish for this right. Mothers were particularly intrigued with the idea; 73% of them (but only 62% of fathers) said they wished they could choose their children's schools. The percentage of public school parents who said they would choose the same schools their children currently attended dropped from the higher 1979 level down to 65%, again with women particularly favoring the change.

In 1987 *all* respondents were asked whether they thought parents in their community should have the right to choose which local school their children would attend. Seventy-one percent of the total sample (and 81% of all nonpublic school parents) said yes; only 20% of the total sample said no.

By 1990 several states had begun experimenting with parental choice plans among public schools, and the idea of school choice had the backing of President Bush and the U.S. Department of Education. The PDK/Gallup question on choice was asked in a new form. As framed in 1989, the question had avoided the issue of public versus nonpublic schools. People were asked simply whether they favored or opposed allowing students and their parents to choose the public schools that students attend, regardless of where they lived. A sizable majority supported the idea in 1989 (60% in favor, 31% opposed), and the results were virtually identical when the same question was asked again in 1990.

In the 1989 poll, the question on school choice was followed by three other questions intended to reveal opinions on whether choice would improve all or only some schools, whether choice would improve student achievement, and whether choice would increase student satisfaction with the local schools. A majority (51%) thought choice would improve some schools and hurt others. Forty-two percent thought that choice would not make much difference in student achievement, while another 40% thought that achievement would increase. About half of the respondents (49%) thought that student satisfaction with the schools would improve; 37% said that choice would make little difference; and 7% said that student satisfaction would be lower.

The 1990 poll added a new dimension to the survey's treatment of parental choice. Respondents were asked what aspects of a public school would be most influential in their decision making should parental choice be adopted in their community. Teacher quality, student discipline, and the curriculum were judged to be very important by three-fourths of all respondents; but class size, the track record of graduates in college or on the job, school size, and proximity to the student's home also were rated either very or fairly important by large majorities.

Parental choice in public education raises the same question that critics of voucher systems raise: Would not parental choice encourage or permit segregation on the basis of race, ethnicity, and socioeconomic status? Forty-eight percent of the 1990 respondents admitted that the racial or ethnic composition of the student body would be either a very or a fairly important consideration in their decision about which school their children would attend. But the response put racial and ethnic considerations near the bottom of the list.

However, in interpreting such data it is well to remember the distinction drawn between public opinion and private sentiment by historian John Lukacs: Public opinion is the formal remarks that respondents make to pollsters; private sentiment is the set of beliefs and biases that people often are too embarrassed to disclose. It is possible that racial and ethnic considerations are more important factors in school choice than people admit to pollsters.

When the question of factors in school choice was repeated in the 1991 poll, the results were almost identical, except that this time racial and ethnic composition of the student body was dead last among factors considered. Whereas in 1990, 48% of the respondents said that race/ethnicity would be either very important (21%) or fairly important (27%) in their choice of schools, in 1991 the figures dropped to 14% and 18% respectively, a total of 32%.

Some students of the poll wondered just what respondents had in mind when they said that racial and ethnic composition of the student body would be important in respondents' decisions. To probe this issue further, the 1991 poll included several follow-up questions. One asked about the ideal percentage of whites to have in a school, one was an open-ended question asking why racial and ethnic composition was important, one asked whether it is very important or fairly important that there not be "too many" members of racial and ethnic minorities in a school, and one asked whether it is very important or fairly important that there not be "too few" members of these groups.

Only 3% of whites said that the schools ideally should be 100% white, and an identical percentage of nonwhites said that schools should enroll no whites at all. In reply to the open-ended "why" question, the most common response (made by one-third of respondents) was, "It is important to have a balanced racial mix." On the final question, 9% of whites said there were too many minority students in their local public schools; 13% said there were too few. Blacks, on the other hand, were somewhat less satisfied with the status quo. Thirty percent of blacks said there were too few minority students in the schools, 15% said too many, and 29% said about the right number.

If parents were offered a choice among the public schools of their community or region and were looking for the school best suited for their offspring, they would need to know not only their children's needs but which schools might best meet those needs. Just how difficult a task would this be, and how well prepared for it is the typical parent? To probe in this matter, poll planners in 1991 devised a set of four questions, as follows, asked of parents with children in public schools.

1. If you could choose your children's schools among many of the public schools in this community, would you choose the ones they now attend or different ones?

	National Totals
	%
Would choose same as now	68
Different ones	23
Don't know	9

Compared with the small numbers who actually make changes in the states where choice is permitted, the 23% figure above is intriguing. Perhaps it means that in the future more parents will begin making changes.

To determine whether parents would be well enough informed to make wise decisions in choosing a school, parents were then asked how much they knew about the advantages and disadvantages of the schools in their community, whether they felt they had enough information to make a wise choice and, if not, how difficult they felt it would be to obtain this information. About one-third (33%) said they knew little or nothing at all about the schools; 39% felt they did not have enough information to make a wise choice. Of the latter group, 44% thought this kind of information would be "very difficult" or "fairly difficult" to obtain.

2. How much would you say you know about the advantages and disadvantages of the different public schools in this community — a great deal, a fair amount, very little, or nothing at all?

	National Totals
	%
A great deal	19
A fair amount	43
Very little	29
Nothing at all	4
No response	5

3. Suppose you could choose any school in this school district. Do you feel you have enough information about the different public

schools in this community to make the best choice for your child, or not?

	National Totals %
Yes, know enough	51
No, don't know enough	39
Don't know	10

4. How difficult do you think it would be to obtain this kind of information — very difficult, fairly difficult, not too difficult, or not difficult at all? (This question was asked of those who felt they did not have enough information to make the best choice.)

	National Totals %
Very difficult	8
Fairly difficult	36
Not too difficult	42
Not difficult at all	7
Don't know	7

These parental responses suggest the difficulties that can arise when parents are allowed to choose the public schools their children attend. Clearly, many people are not sure they have — or even could easily get — the kind of information about schools that would make good choices possible.

CONCLUSION

Pauline Gough, writing the Editor's Page for the September 1990 *Phi Delta Kappan*, asked a basic question about polling public attitudes toward public education. First, she noted discrepancies between public perceptions and school realities. For example, the American public frequently has identified discipline as the number-one problem facing the schools, she said. But teacher surveys during the same years ranked discipline far down the list. Teachers know that unacceptable behavior in school results from some missing elements in kids' environment, and those missing elements are the real problem.

In 1986 poll respondents lifted drug abuse into the number-one position among school problems, just as the University of Michigan surveys were showing a decline in drug abuse among high school youngsters. Only 29 of 830 respondents in a teacher poll conducted by Phi Delta Kappa in 1989 mentioned drug abuse as a problem in their schools.

Gough concluded that a majority of the annual PDK/Gallup poll respondents are naive observers who lack firsthand information about the schools. "Indeed," she wrote, "when respondents were asked in 1988 where they got their information about schools, the largest number (52%) said they relied on newspapers — up from 38% in 1973, when the largest number said they relied on students for their information." (The change reflects a drop in the proportion of adults who have children in school.)

"So why bother with the annual poll?" Gough asked (rhetorically, of course — she published a 15-page report of the 22nd annual poll in the same issue). "The answer," she said, "is that public perceptions — accurate or not — are important to school people. Knowledge of public opinion helps us do a better job." She gave some examples:

> When public opinion is clearly in error (as is the case this year regarding the connection between retention in grade and dropping out), we must try to educate the public.

When public opinion suggests that a widely touted innovation may have anticipated negative consequences (as is the case this year regarding the possible effects of school choice on the racial composition of student bodies), we must pay attention to that finding and make certain that the negative consequences do not materialize.

When the public expresses its opinion on policy or on curriculum and instruction, we must listen carefully — and respond, after conducting local polls to make sure that national opinion tallies with local sentiment.

When public opinion suggests that the schools have an image problem, we must take steps to improve that image.

And when the grades that *parents* give the schools suggest that familiarity breeds respect, we must not only take that important lesson to heart — but also take heart from it.

Phi Delta Kappa was extremely lucky to inherit a poll whose guiding genius was the late George Gallup, Sr. Not only was he the father of scientific polling and a master of polling techniques, Gallup also was vitally interested in education, and he was a man of unquestioned integrity. While people have questioned the usefulness of some of the questions posed in the poll and sometimes their wording, no one, so far as I know, has ever questioned the objectivity of the poll or the motives of its sponsors.

In a golden anniversary edition of *Esquire* magazine, published in December 1983, Gallup was one of some 50 persons honored for their contributions to America in the 20th century. He was called a "trailblazer," along with eight others, among them Jonas Salk and Alfred Kinsey. The introduction to "George Gallup's Nation of Numbers" said this:

> Using methodical means, George Gallup made it possible to know what the people are thinking, issue by issue, moment to moment. Before Gallup, democracy was an exercise in guesswork: letters from constituents, the results of infrequent elections. Elected officials can now feel the public pulse more accurately, and one might assume they have become more sensitive to the voters' wishes. Gallup's methods also changed marketing: product testing and advertising campaigns are only two of the areas that today are dependent on how the numbers come out. Indeed, statistics is now unto itself big business. And George Gallup is its Henry Ford.

George Gallup died in Switzerland on 27 July 1984, just days after writing a report of the 16th Phi Delta Kappa/Gallup education poll for the *Phi Delta Kappan*. Since then his younger son, Alec, has demonstrated the same devotion to the poll, usually collaborating with an educator in the report that is presented in the *Kappan*. Among polling organizations that now number, by one estimate, more than 300 in the United States alone, the Gallup Organization has preserved its reputation for accuracy and integrity. It continues to bottle the air of democracy — the stuff that a British prime minister, Sir Robert Peel, once called "that great compound of folly, weakness, prejudice, wrong feeling, right feeling, obstinacy, and newspaper paragraphs which is called public opinion." What Montaigne called "unmeasurable." And what Alexis de Tocqueville called "the dominant power."

George Gallup was himself less grandiloquent: "If government is supposed to be based on the will of the people," he said, "then somebody ought to go out and find what that will is."

Now, for more than a quarter-century, the PDK/Gallup polls have attempted to honor this view with regard to the public's opinions about their public schools.

REFERENCES

Berliner, D.C. "Mythology and the American System of Education." In *The State of the Nation's Public Schools: A Conference Report*, edited by S. Elam. Bloomington, Ind.: Phi Delta Kappa, 1993.

Coleman, J.S. "Reflections on Schools and Adolescents." In *Reflections: Personal Essays by 33 Distinguished Educators*, edited by D. Burleson. Bloomington, Ind.: Phi Delta Kappa Educational Foundation, 1991.

Cookson, P. *School Choice: The Struggle for the Soul of American Education*. New Haven, Conn.: Yale University Press, 1994.

Jordan, K.F., and Lyons, T.S. *Financing Public Education in an Era of Change*. Bloomington, Ind.: Phi Delta Kappa Educational Foundation, 1992.

Kaplan, G. *Images of Education: The Mass Media's Version of America's Schools*. Washington, D.C.: Institute for Educational Leadership, 1992.

Levin, H. "The Theory of Choice Applied to Education." In *Choice and Control in American Education*, edited by W.H. Clune and J.F. Witte. Bristol, Pa.: Falmer Press, 1990.

Lieberman, M. *Public Education: An Autopsy*. Cambridge, Mass.: Harvard University Press, 1993.

U.S. Bureau of the Census. *Poverty in the United States: 1991*. Current Population Reports, Series P.60, No. 181. Washington, D.C., 1993.

Woodring, P. *The Persistent Problems of Education*. Bloomington, Ind.: Phi Delta Kappa Educational Foundation, 1983.

APPENDIX

HOW TO
DO YOUR OWN POLL:
PHI DELTA KAPPA'S
PACE MATERIALS

Soon after Phi Delta Kappa began publishing full reports of the annual Gallup Poll of the Public's Attitudes Toward the Public Schools in the early Seventies, fraternity leaders recognized that the worth of the poll might be enhanced if an economical but effective local polling method could be developed and disseminated. Local polls not only would enable school districts and other agencies to compare attitudes in smaller geographic areas with national opinion on a variety of school-related topics, but they also would give policy makers insights into education problems and concerns particular to a geographic area or political entity.

It was not until 1980 that a viable method and the tools to implement it became available through Phi Delta Kappa. Wilmer Bugher, then associate executive secretary for administration and head of the PDK Center for the Dissemination of Innovative Programs, had doggedly pursued the idea since the delegates at the 1977 biennial council recommended creating a commission to develop a model for citizen participation and the improvement of public attitudes toward the public schools. Like other fraternity leaders, Bugher was convinced that public esteem for the schools had declined; so he presented PDK Executive Director Lowell Rose with a proposal "to develop a 'how to' manual and supportive materials to aid school personnel in using the Gallup poll questions in polling local community attitudes toward education."

After gaining Rose's approval, Bugher sought the help of polling experts at the Gallup Organization in Princeton, New Jersey. With whole-hearted cooperation from George Gallup, Sr., he got this help. But it was Bugher himself, with the editorial assistance of Willard Duckett, who drafted and refined the first PACE manual. PACE stands for Polling Attitudes of the Community on Education. The manual, which is updated regularly, is composed of chapters on:

- constructing the questionnaire,
- classifying the questions used in the annual PDK/Gallup education polls,
- selecting the sample,
- training interviewers, and
- analyzing the data.

In addition to the manual, PACE materials now include two handbooks for interviewers, one for face-to-face interviewing and one for telephone surveys. (It has been found in recent years that telephone polls are no longer subject to the economic bias that once rendered them invalid.) There also is a 55-minute videotape focusing on appropriate and inappropriate techniques for conducting a personal interview.

When he studied the first PACE manual, Dr. Gallup was very favorably impressed. He said, "This is unique. It is the first time anyone has put together, in one package, complete instructions for the nonspecialist on how to conduct scientific polls of attitude and opinion on education."

In fact, the manual also provides a process for polling attitudes of any group on subjects other than education. Robert Mauller, a now-retired Los Angeles Unified Schools administrator, recently wrote, "I have never found any other source that describes in detail each step that is necessary to develop, conduct, and measure a poll. Obviously, the questions have to be changed, but the underlying principles for framing questions remain the same. The manual is a road map to successful determination of attitudes, which is far better than just listening to people argue." Mauller has used the PACE manual successfully in three situations in Los Angeles. He described one instance as follows:

> At one time the Unified School District was considering closing its PBS television station, mainly for budgetary reasons. A supporting argument was that teachers did not seem to use the channel for instructional purposes. One board member was particularly concerned and challenged me to provide a better estimate of how many teachers used the channel, what programs, how often, and at what grade level. She was referring to the Nielsen reports, which were not available for such a small station as ours and in any case would be far too expensive to purchase. She required an answer in three weeks.
>
> I used PACE and was able to provide a response in the allotted time. The board had difficulty in accepting the report findings and said my procedures must be faulty. The district's Internal Audit Unit, which was directly responsible to the board, was ordered to conduct an investigation of my process. Its review took twice as

long as my poll had taken but it verified the accuracy of my findings.

The result was that the PBS station was saved and the board
learned to appreciate what it provided students. They even went
further, beginning to use it themselves to broadcast board meet-
ings.

PACE is a marvelous manual and is a basic item in my library.
I hope many others will take advantage of its availability.

Actually, many people have already done so. In all, Phi Delta Kappa
has distributed some 3,100 PACE manuals and related materials. Although the Dissemination Center does not maintain a library of school
district poll reports, PDK officials do know that four statewide polls
have been taken using the PACE materials. These states are Maryland
(twice), Indiana, and North Carolina.

Although the PACE program is regarded as self-instructional, the
PDK Dissemination Center will consult with PACE users according to
their needs. As an example, where users have difficulty in analyzing
their data, the center can provide electronic scoring of results.

Persons interested in knowing more about the PACE materials should
write to Phi Delta Kappa, P.O. Box 789, Bloomington, IN 47402-0789,
or telephone (812) 339-1156 or 1-800-766-1156.